When The Pain Sets In: A Devotion For Dealing With Loss

Ariel Henderson

Thank You

Bryant

Thank you for being the promise that I needed. God said that you would help me heal, and you have done just that. I love you always.

Joshua and Harper

You two are the fuel I need every day. You remind me to keep living and loving. Never lose the joy that's in the twinkle in your eyes. All my love.

Mom

Thank You for every encouraging word, prayer and meal. You supported me with the kids even though you were suffering with your own pain.

Tink

I appreciate all the hugs you have given. You are wiser than you know. I love you.

Mama Alice

Thank You for blessing me with your daughter. Thank You for accepting me as apart of your family. I am forever grateful.

To My Sisters and Other Mothers

Thank You for being supportive and holding my arms up during this battle. I Am grateful that we get to do life together. I appreciate y'all.

Contents

Before You Read

It has taken 6 years to write this devotional. I have lived every word, cried, fought, and asked why a million times. I contemplated taking my own life, but God knew I would run into you. Whoever you are and whatever place you are in, I hope this body of work will be refreshing to you. Even if you are at the edge don't forget that someone is waiting to meet you. They need the testimony that you will develop.

Touch the person reading this book. He/She is looking for answers from you. Answers that only your whispers can provide. As they read each page, heal them and love them. Be what you know they need from you and you alone! In Jesus Name

Defaming
The
Myth Of Grief

Death is something that unifies us all. It will happen to each and every one of us. Most times, we fear what we don't understand. In this devotional, it is my goal to help you become victorious over death and take out the life lessons to help you get the most of your time while you're still here.

What We Think It Is: The Myth Behind What We Fear

Naturally, we like to be in control. But what happens when one thing that you can't control is right in your face? Death is something that most of us run from, try to buy away, or even block out.

There is so much that pain can teach us about ourselves. When a person we love passes on does their shadow leave a mark? Does the lack of their presence put you in a cage or backed into a corner?

I fought to keep the thoughts of death away. I would try to "keep God" pleased by reading my bible all the time and praying 3 times a day. I thought that if I could be perfect then God would keep death away from me and those that I loved. I lived in constant fear and dread of death.I didn't want to understand it. But I would learn that God had different plans. I would like to sit down and share the different levels of grief I've experienced. Y'all, it was no joke.

In 2014 I went through so many transitions it made my head spin. My great-grandmother passed, but she lived to see almost 90, so we were prepared for her passing. Our family knew that her time was coming, and we were at peace with that. A few weeks later, I found out I was pregnant.

The same week my mother told my grandfather, who was in the hospital at the time. Before I go on, let me explain my relationship with my grandparents. They meant so much to me. I was their first grandchild, and I was always with them. They planted seeds and watched me grow.

Losing someone that you love is an earth-shattering experience. Its very existence is assigned to bring us to God our Father, who comforts and is close to the brokenhearted **(Psalms 34:18),** But what do we do while our heart is still broken?

What can I learn from this moment? When my best friend died, I had to wonder who I was. All over again, my identity was being reshaped. Even though I am married and have love all around, no-one can fill this space or make the pain

go away.

"Show me who I am now through the lens of this pain. You said you would be a comfort, so I ask you to love me into shape. Love me into life, love me into your image.

In Jesus Name".

Who was I before My Loved One Died?
Who Am I Now Without Them?

_____

_____

_____

_____

_____

_____

_____

_____

_____

_____

_____

_____

_____

_____

_____

_____

_____

_____

Coping With Grief

When a person passes you don't just grieve their lives. Depending on how important the connection was between you and that person, you grieve their influence in your own life. You grieve "what do I do now"? You ask God, "how do I reorganize life now that this person is not here?" Death changes life's routines. It changes your perspective and can propel you for the better if you choose to let Christ lead you through the affliction, loss and pain.

God has used this process to change my surroundings. I am aware of the relationships that are important to have around. Everything that I was familiar with also changed, and God began removing the training wheels. I searched in my heart and asked, "Do I trust you to take care of me?" Can I trust you to lead me out of this pain or has my trust been in the loved one that I hurt for?

When my best friend passed, I kept asking God what am I gonna do next? I was in complete shock, numbness and disbelief. Is that you right now? Can you relate to how that feels? I believe there are different levels of pain that brings out a certain response that God is looking for. It is a cup of trust that he can meet alone.

"Dealing with your emotions when grieving the loss of someone you love is a fight within itself."

Trusting you turns the mirror on me

"Grieving is a constant reflectional journey. The reflection is like a cocoon, and after you bloom, you become a whole new person".

I invite you to look back on their passing and ask:

How did they play a part in your life?

_____

_____

_____

_____

_____

_____

_____

_____

_____

_____

_____

_____

_____

_____

_____

_____

_____

_____

_____

_____

_____

_____

_____

_____

_____

_____

_____

_____

_____

_____

_____

_____

_____

_____

_____

_____

_____

_____

Were they foundational or key instruments in your progress?

_____

_____

_____

_____

_____

_____

_____

_____

_____

_____

_____

_____

_____

_____

_____

_____

_____

_____

_____

What did they teach you and what did you keep?

_____

_____

_____

_____

_____

_____

_____

_____

_____

_____

_____

_____

_____

_____

_____

_____

_____

_____

What will you use that they instilled in you?

_____

_____

_____

_____

_____

_____

_____

_____

_____

_____

_____

_____

_____

_____

_____

_____

_____

_____

_____

Thoughts

_____

_____

_____

_____

_____

_____

_____

_____

_____

_____

_____

_____

_____

_____

_____

_____

_____

_____

_____

_____

_____

_____

_____

_____

_____

_____

_____

_____

_____

_____

_____

_____

_____

_____

_____

_____

_____

_____

_____

_____

_____

Cocoon

Of Reflection

This is the transition from relying on that person to fully trusting God. This makes the cocoon break and allows you to fly."

When reflecting on your loved one it's important to:

Ask Questions

What did they teach you?

Grieve Your Ability

Can I do this without them?

Make a decision to be truthful with God and yourself.

Be fully willing and ready to trust God.

My
Grief Story

My Grandfather: The Mind

My grandfather was always the puzzle piece that helped lay a foundation. My father wasn't really present. But paw-paw was. If you knew my family, then you would know that we had some good times, and some things looked like a scene from a movie, lol. We grew up baptist, and my grandfather was the pastor of a church in Memphis, Tn.

Even though he was a pastor and he made so many mistakes, I learned how to treat people with love and kindness because of him. He was nicknamed "The gentle giant" because he had a powerful and quiet presence. The most impactful value he gave me was nurturing my mind. He always encouraged me to never lose "wonder" in God, in life, and in myself. My grandfather was the type to give you wisdom if you asked for it. He taught me that what you do with your mind is key.

My Grandmother: The Heart

Now Nana was the ball of fire, lol. I spent most if not all of my time with my grandparents. I was the first grandchild, and I had a special connection to them. I didn't understand it then, but I cherish it now. Nana taught me how to be a servant. I learned how to have a heart from her because she nourished my heart. She would come alive when she expressed herself through decorating.

She loved giving and being invested in the hearts of others. Y'all, when I tell y'all that this woman would not sit down, she was always doing something for somebody.

I often ask God why our relationship turned out the way it did. My mother's relationship with her mother was full of hardships, questions and pain. But towards the end of her life, I am glad that my mother and I spent the last weekend of her life with her.

Sheena: The Spirit

The first time I met Sheena, we clashed. I was a 20- year-old who felt like I didn't need any help or guidance. Sheena was older than me, so she felt the same way. She didn't want to mentor anyone because she was afraid to trust. She had been hurt by others in her life, and declining was a way of protecting herself.

So, you could imagine the clashing that took place when God brought us together in friendship. I thought I knew who God was until he showed me that I had much to learn! Sheena wasn't the type for nonsense because anytime I had a question about God and it required research, she would always tell me to look it up. Our mentorship grew into a sisterhood. It took many years of labor for her to trust me enough to call me family. But that hard exterior melted away in both of our hearts. It was through the many adventures we had together that drew me closer to Christ.

The Holy Spirit became family throughout our relationship together. Sheena and I had the type of connection that David and Johnathan had. Their spirits were intertwined, and so were ours. She became everything God knew I needed, and he used her to nurture my spirit. There were certain places that were not opened in my life until the power of relationship gave me access to Christ in a way I had never experienced before. But our relationship suffered a bit when she found out that she had cancer. Instead of life falling apart, we learned the ends and outs of God's grace through the doctors' appointments, chemo and surgeries.

We talked about her passing a lot (she talked and I rebutted) I thought we would have more time to share other adventures, but on January 3 of 2017, the Lord called her home. And to be honest, my heart still doesn't believe it. I looked for her text or phone call. I was often angry and in a state of shock a lot. I mean we were preparing for one day but 3 days into the new year.. God really! That's what I thought. I didn't believe I would be brave enough to handle life without my best friend. But because of her death, this book came to life. She inspired every page because the legacy she left behind were seeds of passion, fullness and purpose.

So what seeds/tools did your loved one leave or give you to succeed? Ask yourself, what ground do you want to plant those seeds in? It is still painful not being able to see or hear from my grandparents and my best friend. But God blessed me with 3 wonderful people who helped lay the foundation of who I am in Christ. Without them taking the time to lay down the bricks they did, I don't know who would have been.

Live the life that will leave greatness behind even when someone mentions your name, God's glory rolls off their tongue. Make time for your family and friends, get closure where you need it. Even if the closure involves the person that passed, give it to God and let him close that chapter for you through his healing power. Take what you learned through your own grieving and share and empower others. Before you know it you'll be a part of someone's adventure, and they will thank you for it.

How I Coped
With Losing
Loved One's

When my grandparents died, I felt like I was sinking. I was screaming for help, and no one could help me, not even God! I was a pregnant newlywed who was depressed because of the changes that were happening around me. I didn't want to seek counseling. Why should I? I know what they were going to say, I thought. It is normal going through stages, but grief takes a turn when you try to take on that pain yourself.

How I coped with losing loved one's I experienced:

Anger
God why did you let this happen?

Sadness/Disbelief
What am I supposed to do now? How can this hole in my heart be filled?

Isolation
"I'm okay,I just don't want to talk right now"

Comfort/Deliverance
God was patient in every part of my brokenness. Even when I didn't understand. I experienced peace like never before.

Tired
"I just want to sleep the day away"

Change in Perspective
Why is my life important? What can I do to add value to my life and other's ?

Unity in a heavy heart

(Excerpt from my journal)

04-19-17

"One moment I am fine, and then months later I am in disbelief and shock again! How am I supposed to keep going like nothing ever happened? Like Sheena never existed. I want to call and talk to you, but then I realize I can only see you in my memories, thoughts and dreams. God HELP"0-!

What do you want to say to the person you love? Let your heart flow and write a letter to your loved one. It helps in the process of healing.

Thoughts

How Did God Deal With Grief: When Grief First Started

In order to answer this question in full detail, we must travel back to the beginning. When life was sweet, and there was no end to the connection between God and his first love. What happens when love turns sour and conceives disobedience? **Grief is born**!

God's idea was for us to be in a companionship. Can you imagine everything you worked hard to build turns upside down and is unrecognizable within a matter of seconds?

How Does God Deal With His Pain?

1.

He looks for himself
Feeling the disconnection God's anxious heart looks for Adam and Eve

(He looks for his image)

Genesis 3:8-11

2.

Confronts the issue What did you do and why?

Genesis 3:8-11

3.

Makes a resolution
He decides how he would fix the situation.

(He sent grace ahead of time.)

Grief Through History

What can we learn from Peter

Peter was the closest friend to Jesus and shared many intimate moments with him. You would think that those moments would change and transform him, right? Nope! Peter's transformation did not come into full effect until Jesus died. The full effect couldn't happen until there was enough space (room) in Peter to be filled from the inside out. It would have been nice if Jesus continued their relationship the way they did, but Jesus would have only become a crutch or a dependent to Peter. That's the opposite of what Jesus wanted to be for him. He didn't want to become a religion to him, but he came to build a relationship with him. In order for that to happen, Jesus had to die. He had to leave Peter uncomfortable tossing and turning with the lessons, memories, teachings and adventures they shared together. What do you do when you can't fill that place in your stomach that is yearning for that comfort you once knew when your loved one was still here?

Peter tried to cope. He held on to the last piece of instruction that Jesus left him, hoping that he would experience him again. But Peter began to loose hope, and an outpouring of grief flowed out that he possibly never experienced or could put into words. In order for Peter to be filled again, he had to receive the Holy Spirit and release everything that was in him truthfully and painfully. Sometimes, we don't understand why God allows the pain of loss to feel so full and unrestricted. But it is the realness of this pain that purifies us from the inside out. This moment leaves no room for doubt, worry, fear, ANYTHING! It uproots and leaves no rock unturned, allowing us to be clear and positioned to take the next steps from God. Peter was able to appreciate and take in every moment that happened and would happen. His experience with Jesus was clear and understood. This moment also fueled his passion for his purpose. Any lack of understanding, wandering and wondering ended when the Holy Spirit partnered with him.

The Legacy We Leave Behind

Death is a subject that many of us don't want to talk about. We disregard it and keep it silent, hoping it's a bad dream and it will go away. Allow courage to settle in your heart. It didn't hit me this way until my grandmother passed. Here I am with all of these new blessings in my life, but I had no idea how to manage them, teach them to my family and live in it. It is important to sit down and talk about what happens after you pass. Sooner or later, we will all hear Jesus make that call for us. But allow peace to settle in your heart because being with Jesus in full will always be home.

Definition of Legacy: anything handed down from the past,as from an ancestor to predecessor.

So, what do you want to pass down to your children? What legacy do you want to leave them with? Don't leave the ones you love with empty questions that you can fill in for them right now. A legacy doesn't always mean money, but in this case, what impact do you desire to leave behind? Will the world know greatness in the way you lived and loved? Or will the world carry on as if you don't exist? Issac is a perfect example of what a great legacy can be (we are still talking about him today) Sarah and Abraham passed down some amazing values, adventures and life skills that prepared Issac to carry the paton.

Sarah lived an authentic life.

She learned how to trust God and her husband. Part of her legacy was how she carried her marriage, how she honored her first husband (God), and how she submitted to her second (Abraham). Make no mistake, there was nothing perfect about how she got to this place, but it was enough to inspire Isaac with his wife.

"Isaac brought her into the tent of his mother Sarah, and he married Rebekah. So she became his wife and he loved her and Issac was comforted after his mother's death." (Genesis 24:67)

 The jewel in this scripture was that Issac was comforted. His mother left a legacy of a beautiful marriage and it was passed down to him. Marriage brings comfort after death. That is God's blessing to those who are married.

Abraham

Issac's father was the pillar of hope and of faith. He trusted God even when he had no clue that his plans existed. What propels the legacy is how Issac saw his father. He watched him cry out, he saw him through his adventures and believed in him during the test. Because of Abraham's relationship with God Issac walked through an open door of blessings. The legacy Abraham paved and

left behind for Issac was **obedience!**

After Abraham's death,God blessed his son Issac, who then lived near Beer Lahai Roi. **Genesis 25:11**

Jesus

And then there is Jesus! The superhero above all supers! The entire bible is fashioned, geared toward the legacy of Christ. Could you imagine asking God what legacy he wanted to leave behind, and in an instant, you see Jesus enduring a terrible death but an even greater resurrection. In that resurrection, he had you in mind. You are the legacy. When he created you, he created endless possibilities of hope, love, joy etc. They dwell inside of us. His light belongs to us, his peace is ours, his friendship is priceless and the material stuff is just a bonus. **(Romans 8:35)** You are God's most precious creation! He breathed legacy into you. What are you going to do with that authority?

Thoughts

Legacy

Live a life that will leave greatness behind even when someone mentions your name, God's glory rolls off their tongue. Make time for your family and friends, get closure where you need it even if the closure involves the person that passed. Give it to him and let Jesus close that chapter for you through healing. Take what you learned through your own grieving and share and empower others. Before you know it, you'll be a part of someone's adventure, and they will thank you for it!

The Legacy Pact

The legacy pact is designed to help you move in the direction that powers a better life in Christ while you're living and when you pass on. May these questions put death and life in kingdom perspective for you and those around you.

Answer only when you are ready to be open and honest with God and yourself. Choose someone who will hold you accountable and walk this pact out with them.

My Accountability Partner is

What type of life are you living?

Would your loved one's be full and whole from the life you lead?

_____

_____

_____

_____

_____

_____

_____

_____

_____

_____

_____

_____

_____

_____

_____

_____

_____

_____

_____

_____

Would they be inspired by your light?

_____

_____

_____

_____

_____

_____

_____

_____

_____

_____

_____

_____

_____

_____

_____

_____

_____

_____

_____

_____

_____

I want to live a life of?

My legacy that I will pass on is?

_____

_____

_____

_____

_____

_____

_____

_____

_____

_____

_____

_____

_____

_____

_____

_____

_____

_____

Do You have Life Insurance?

Do You have a living will?

_____

_____

_____

_____

_____

_____

_____

_____

_____

_____

_____

_____

_____

_____

_____

_____

_____

_____

_____

If needed My Power of Attorney is?

_____

_____

_____

_____

_____

_____

_____

_____

_____

_____

_____

_____

_____

_____

_____

_____

_____

_____

Who will get guardianship over my children?

_____

_____

_____

_____

_____

_____

_____

_____

_____

_____

_____

_____

_____

_____

_____

_____

_____

_____

_____

Funeral Arrangements / Celebration of Life

Color/ outfit I want to be buried in

_____

_____

_____

_____

_____

_____

_____

_____

_____

_____

_____

_____

_____

_____

_____

_____

_____

_____

_____

_____

Place where I want my life to be celebrated

_____

_____

_____

_____

_____

_____

_____

_____

_____

_____

_____

_____

_____

_____

_____

_____

_____

_____

_____

_____

What would you want your family and loved one's to know

_____

_____

_____

_____

_____

_____

_____

_____

_____

_____

_____

_____

_____

_____

_____

_____

_____

_____

Do you have a relationship With Christ?

_____

_____

_____

_____

_____

_____

_____

_____

_____

_____

_____

_____

_____

_____

_____

_____

_____

_____

_____

It is important to have all of your key information and documents filed in a place where your beneficiary can utilize it when needed.

Life Insurance Beneficiary

Power Of Attorney

Username

Password

Username

Password

Balm For Your Wounds: Scriptures To Help You Say What You Need

Renewal

Grief is a shattering experience, ask God for renewal.

_____

_____

Psalm 51:10

Create pure thoughts in me and make me faithful again.

_____

_____

Foundation

Even when we don't understand, and knowing who he is to us is the foundation of our strength. It is where we start to heal.

_____

_____

Psalms 18:2

You are my mighty rock, my fortress, my protector, the rock where I am safe, my shield, my powerful weapon, and my place of shelter.

Psalms 28:7

You are my strong shield, and I trust you completely. You have helped me, and I will celebrate and thank you in song.

Psalms 71:1

I run to you, LORD, for protection. Don't disappoint me.

Comfort

When we feel alone he is always with us.

_____

_____

Deuteronomy 31:8

The LORD will lead you into the land. He will always be with you and help you, so don't ever be afraid of your enemies.

Jeremiah 29:12-13

You will turn back to me and ask for help, and I will answer your prayers. You will worship me with all your heart, and I will be with you.

_____

_____

Strength

Putting everything in his hands takes time. But it is the process that solidifies you.

_____

_____

Joshua 1:9

I've commanded you to be strong and brave. Don't ever be afraid or discouraged! I am the LORD your God, and I will be there to help you wherever you go.

Ephesians 5:2

Let love be your guide. Christ loved us and offered his life for us as a sacrifice that pleases God.

Psalm 33:4

The LORD is truthful; he can be trusted.

Hope

This ignites and empowers you.

_____

_____

1 Thessalonians 4:13-18

My friends, we want you to understand how it will be for those followers who have already died. Then you won't grieve over them and be like people who don't have any hope. We believe Jesus died and was raised to life. We also believe that when God brings Jesus back again, he will bring with him all who had faith in Jesus before they died.

Our Lord Jesus told us that when he comes, we won't go up to meet him ahead of his followers who have already died. With a loud command and with the shout of the chief angel and a blast of God's trumpet, the Lord will return from heaven.

Then those who had faith in Christ before they died will be raised to life. Next, all of us who are still alive will be taken up into the clouds together with them to meet the Lord in the sky. From that time on we will all be with the Lord forever. Encourage each other with these words.

_____

_____

1 Thessalonians 5:10

Christ died for us, so we could live with him, whether we are alive or dead when he comes.

Unity

In

Release

Below is a set of prayers made out to you from people who have also dealt with the pain and journey of losing someone. I invite you to pray these prayers as much as you need. Know that you are not alone, and we are always praying for you. We are in this together.

Loss of a loved one

Lord we know that though there is healing and comfort. At the moment nothing seems to be able to help the loss they feel. Their heart is broken and their spirit mourns. So father, I ask you to send your peace to them. Continue to surround them with those who will offer words of comfort.

Give them sweet and restful sleep. Father remove the heaviness, and give them a heart of praise. Father I ask that you will bless their lives to overflow with laughter and joy again.

As they take refuge in you please help them to put their trust in you. Holy Spirit we ask that you settle the hearts and minds of those who are feeling any guilt, resentment, bitterness and anger. Help them not to look back but press forward in and with you. Father continue to surround them with your peace and love that surpasses all things.

And in Jesus name we pray

Amen.

For the one who Grieves

Touch and hear those who are having a hard time releasing. Create an atmosphere where their heart is safe enough to cry out to you. You said that they are blessed even right now through this time of hardship and trial. Let their heart pour out to you in truth, so they can be filled and fueled by you.

In Jesus Name

Loss of a Spouse
by Aaron Johnson

Our father, thank you for the many blessings you have so freely given to us, one and all. We stand before you now, asking for your continued leadership and direction as we travel through life this day. As our spouse has graduated from this life on earth, we look to you to direct our course, guide our feet and illuminate our path through the remainder of this life journey.

In Jesus name amen

Loss of a Father
By Pamela Henderson (Matthew 5:4)

Father, I pray that you be the father to the one who longs for their earthly fathers. I pray that you never let them forget the love and joy their fathers brought them. Lead them to a peace that only you can give Lord. I ask that you be the strength that they need during this time. Let them know that you are always with them when they don't feel you or understand why.

In Jesus name

Loss of a Mother

By Pamela Henderson (Psalms 147:3)

Father, I pray that each person who has lost a mother will be comforted at this moment. I pray they think about the good times and the wisdom that their mother imparted in them. I pray that you let our Lord Jesus Christ wrap his arms around you and comfort you during this time.

In Jesus name

Siblings

By Pamela Henderson (Lamentations 3:21-23)

Father God, now that both our parents are no longer here, I pray for the siblings that are left to deal with their pain, their loneliness, their anger and hurt. Father God I ask you to bring us closer together and not let us be divided apart. I Know we grieve differently but I am thankful that you love us the same. As we rely on each other let us not forget it is you that we all come to. Thank you for unconditional love.

In Jesus Name

Loss of a friend

By Jasonda Habersham

A friend sticks closer than a brother, but I feel like my heart is broken. Lord, I am not sure what I need right now, but I ask that you fill every need that I can't explain. I still love you, but I am angry. Help me work through it. I am still following you, but I can't see the path we're on. And I am afraid of who I will become in the midst of this pain. Help me rediscover who I am moving forward.

In Jesus name

Fears Death

Lord, I am fearful of death. I Have experienced so much loss that I don't know how to come back from this. Teach me how to have a full life. Remove the fear of death and it's thoughts from the garden of my heart and life.

In Jesus Name

Unresolved feelings

Touch me Lord I'm dealing with some ungratefulness, unresolved emotions and hurt. I Don't know how to release this weight in my heart. Father be my strength, be my joy and set me free.
In Jesus Name

Wisdom from a Teenager
By Dominique Miller

Maybe you have lost someone through death. Maybe even a bond was lost. Just know you are not alone. I know that it may be hard to see the reason for them being removed from your life, but there is a plan in the mix. I know it may be hard to ask for help from others or even God at times but have a conversation with him. He already knows what you need. He's just waiting on you to ask. Right now, you are still trying to find yourself at this age, but you can't do it without God. I am not bashing you or anything, nor am I forcing Jesus on you. I just want you to be strong mentally, physically, emotionally and spiritually.

The Promise

I know that the idea of me scares you, or has hurt you. It hurts me to see you in pain, searching and wondering . Know that I see you and know that you matter to me. Before the world came to be, I thought of you. You made my heart skip a beat, I had never felt love like that before. To showcase my love for you I made this promise: I died on the cross for every wrong and hurtful thing you could ever do in your life. As I was buried I waited in anticipation to make you completely mine. Then on the 3rd day I rose with all power in my hands just to give it to you. Do you see how much I love you? Still not convinced? That's okay... I promise to love you past your pain, past your flaws, to include you in my love. I promise that the hurt, pain and bitterness you feel, you will never feel again with me. I will keep you safe. I have promised my life to you will you accept my love?

Jesus loves you more than you know if you want to accept his promise for your life simply say these words: Jesus I accept your promise, I make you mine both now and forever. You are my Lord and Savior, my friend and comfort both now and forever.

˜In Jesus Name˜

So What Now:
Quote From The
Lord Of The
Rings: Return
Of The King

There is a scene in the Lord Of The Rings: Return Of The King that has a powerful healing scene at the end. Sam was called to help his friend Frodo to defeat the evil that wanted to destroy mankind. At the end, Frodo makes a decision to leave middle earth and set sail at sea. He was ready to rest and couldn't go back to the quiet life he once lived. He knew his journey was over and he fulfilled his purpose. This would be the last time his friends would ever see him on earth again.Frodo gives Sam a journal, and on his way home, this is what Frodo says to Sam:

My Dear Sam,
You cannot always be torn in two. You will have to be one and whole for many years. You have so much to enjoy, to be, and to do. Your part of the story will go on.

So, what does that mean for you? If you go through the process of grieving in a healthy way, you have the opportunity to become whole in everything you do and how you live your life from that point on. After you experience death and loss, you are never the same. But I hope that after the pain settles down and the tears become few and far between, you will embrace the wholeness that is being offered to you, and you will be authentic with how you love, how you give and how you share.

Thoughts

_____

_____

_____

_____

_____

_____

_____

_____

_____

_____

_____

_____

_____

_____

_____

_____

_____

_____

_____

_____

_____

_____

_____

Ariel Henderson

_____

_____

_____

_____

_____

_____

_____

_____

_____

_____

_____

_____

_____

_____

_____

_____

_____

_____

_____

_____

_____

_____

_____

_____

_____

_____

_____

_____

_____

_____

_____

_____

_____

_____

_____

_____

_____

_____

_____

_____

_____

_____

_____

_____

_____

_____

_____

_____

_____

_____

_____

_____

_____

_____

_____

_____

_____

_____

_____

_____

_____

_____

_____

About The Author

Ariel is a wife and mother of Joshua and Harper. She has learned how to turn tragedy into triumph. In 2016 she founded Teatime With Nana a ministry and business that was birthed from the devastating loss of her grandmother. With her podcast and life coaching services, Ariel is driven to guide women into becoming their most authentic and complete selves.

Keep In Touch

Website

www.teatimewnana.com

Email

ttwn61@gmail.com

Instagram

@ttwn61

Facebook

Teatime with Nana

Notes

Collins, Harper, ed. "Legacy." Dictionary.com. Dictionary.com, 2012.

https://www.dictionary.com/browse/legacy.

Jackson, Peter. 2003. The Lord of the Rings: The Return of the King. United States: New Line Cinema.

9 781087 857077